T0082172

For Dai
Every robin, wren and house martin
is a message from you.
Thank you for everything.
You are forever in my heart.

Funny Food: Plant-based recipes
Published in Great Britain in 2021 by Graffeg
Limited.

ISBN 9781802580211

Written by Jane Reynolds copyright © 2021.
Food photography by Huw Jones
copyright © 2021.
Post-production by Matt Braham.
Designed and produced by Graffeg Limited
copyright © 2021.

Graffeg Limited, 24 Stradey Park Business
Centre, Mwrwg Road, Llangennech, Llanelli,
Carmarthenshire, SA14 8YP, Wales, UK.
Tel: 01554 824000. www.graffeg.com.

Jane Reynolds is hereby identified as the author
of this work in accordance with section 77 of the
Copyrights, Designs and Patents Act 1988.

A CIP Catalogue record for this book is available
from the British Library.

1 2 3 4 5 6 7 8 9

Funny Food

Plant-based recipes
Jane Reynolds & Huw Jones

GRAFFEG

Contents

Cakes and Desserts

Jane Reynolds

How did the idea of *Funny Food* come about?

I have noticed that there is an increase in popularity of plant-based meals and it's definitely not just for vegans; I know lots of people who want to reduce their intake of meat and dairy, even if it's just a few days a week.

Who did you have in mind when you created these recipes?

Children and teenagers love their food to be fun, so this is for them! Nearly all of the recipes in this book are very easy to make and achievable. I think it is great to get involved in sourcing the ingredients, cooking the dishes and, of course, the very best bit, the eating!

Were your children the first to eat these funny foods?

Lots of these dishes are adapted from recipes and ideas that I used when my children were growing up; they loved

making Welsh cakes, popcorn and anything with noodles or spaghetti. We always loved foraging and going on picnics – food is a great way to celebrate quality time together.

Have you always thought of some foods as funny foods?

When I was growing up, lots of these recipes would have been called 'funny food' because they were considered faddy. Now, in a complete turnaround, a plant-based diet is much more mainstream. I love the title because it is my perception of what makes food funny that has changed so much – it's joyful food that makes me laugh and smile.

Savoury
Snacks

Thingummy Swirly Bob

Thingummy Swirly Bob

Serves 4 | Prep time 40 minutes | Cook time 20 minutes

Ingredients

150g long-grain rice

1 tablespoon rapeseed oil

1 medium onion, peeled and finely diced

50g wild garlic leaves, washed and shredded

170g tub dairy-free soft cheese

230g dairy free feta cheese

Sea salt and black pepper

1 pack of filo pastry

Method

• Put the rice into a medium-sized saucepan with about 320ml of water and a little salt and bring to the boil. Stir once, cover, reduce the heat to a simmer and leave undisturbed for 20 minutes, until all the water has been absorbed. Cool under cold running water, drain and set aside. Preheat the oven to 220°C.

• Heat the oil in a frying pan and gently cook off the onions until they are soft. Stir in the wild garlic until wilted. Turn off the heat. Add in the rice, cream cheese and crumble in the feta. Season with salt and pepper.

• Lay out four sheets of filo pastry, overlapping each sheet by about 2.5cm. Brush with oil and put another layer of filo on top. Brush with oil again.

- Make the filling into a sausage shape along the bottom long edge of the pastry and roll up into a tight roll. Coil into a snail shape, place on a greased baking sheet and bake in the oven for 15-20 minutes until golden and crispy. Decorate with some wild garlic flowers (which are edible), and serve with a spicy dip (such as the one in the spring roll recipe).

- Great for tearing, dipping and sharing!

If wild garlic is not in season, substitute with 100g spinach leaves, nettles, kale, chard or any other leafy greens.

Spring Rolls and Dipping Sauce

Spring Rolls and Dipping Sauce

Makes 15 | Prep time 30 minutes | Cook time 10 minutes

Ingredients

15-20 150 x 150cm spring roll wraps

1 tablespoon rapeseed oil

1 large carrot, peeled and cut into matchsticks

2 cloves garlic, peeled and finely chopped

1 onion, peeled and finely sliced

3 spring onions, finely sliced on the diagonal

½ red pepper, finely diced

75g green cabbage (any sort), finely shredded

150g beansprouts

100g vermicelli

2 teaspoons cornflour

1 tablespoon soya sauce

Vegetable or sunflower oil, for deep frying

To seal the spring rolls

2 teaspoons cornflour

1 tablespoon water

For the dipping sauce

2 teaspoons cornflour

1 tablespoon white wine vinegar

1 tablespoon golden caster sugar

2 tablespoons tomato sauce

2 teaspoons soya sauce

1 teaspoon sriracha

Method

- Heat the oil in a large heavy-based frying pan or wok over high heat.

- Add the carrot, garlic and onions and stir-fry for about 1 minute, stirring all the time, then add the spring onions, pepper and cabbage, stirring often.

- Cover the vermicelli with boiling water, stir and let stand for about 2 minutes.

- Add the bean sprouts and drained vermicelli to the other ingredients, stirring often.

- Mix the cornflour and soya sauce, making sure no lumps remain, and add to the frying pan or wok. Stir for 2-3 minutes. Turn off the heat and allow the filling mixture to cool.

- Mix the cornflour and water together to make a paste to seal the spring rolls with.

Spring Rolls and Dipping Sauce

- Place the spring roll wrappers on the worktop. (One side is slightly shinier than the other – place this side down on the worktop.)

- Place about 1 tablespoon of filling on one of the corners of the wrapper. Fold that corner towards the middle and with a pastry brush apply some of the cornflour mixture to the two outer corners, then fold the sides in to make an envelope.

- Brush the top pointy part of the wrapper, then roll up tightly to make a tube shape.

- Keep the ready-made spring rolls under a damp piece of kitchen roll to prevent them from drying out whilst you assemble the others.

- Heat the vegetable or sunflower oil in a deep fryer or in a large saucepan over medium to high heat.

- Deep fry about 4-5 at a time – don't overcrowd them. Fry for approximately 2-3 minutes until golden brown and crispy. Drain on kitchen roll and keep warm until they are all cooked.

- To make the sauce, mix the cornflour and vinegar together until smooth, then whisk in all the other ingredients. Cook in a small saucepan, stirring often, for 5-6 minutes.

As a youngster, a Chinese takeaway was reserved for very special occasions, and spring rolls are indelibly imprinted into my memory as the epitome of a foodie treat.

Squashage
Rolls

Squashage Rolls

Makes 24 | Prep time 20 minutes | Cook time 40 minutes

Ingredients

2 tablespoons rapeseed oil

2 medium onions, peeled and diced

2 cloves garlic, peeled and finely chopped

½ red pepper, cut into small dice

1 butternut squash, peeled, seeds removed and diced (approximately 350g)

2 medium carrots, peeled and diced

2 medium potatoes, peeled and diced (about 350g)

50g sundried tomatoes, finely chopped

½ teaspoon chilli flakes

1 tablespoon dried mixed herbs

75g walnut pieces

320g pack ready-rolled puff pastry

Splash soya milk

2 teaspoons sesame seeds

Sea salt, freshly ground black pepper, white pepper

Method

- Preheat the oven to 220°C.

- Put the oil in a large roasting tin and spread all the vegetables in an even layer. Season with the chillies and herbs and plenty of sea salt and black pepper. Roast for approximately 30 minutes, or until the vegetables are soft.

- Toast the walnuts for about 5 minutes, keeping a keen eye on them, as they burn easily. Chop the nuts (not too finely) and add to the vegetables.

- With a potato masher or fork, mash the vegetable mixture – it doesn't need to be exceptionally smooth – a few small lumps are fine. Taste and season with more sea salt if needed and some white pepper.

- Set the mixture aside to cool.

- When the mixture is cool, lay the pastry sheet out and cut in half lengthways. Divide the mixture in half and fill the two pastry sheets with a long sausage down the middle of each.

- If there is mixture left over, reserve for later – it is delicious in a sandwich or on toast. Brush one edge of each sheet with soya milk and roll up, keeping the seam underneath. Brush the sausage with soya milk and sprinkle with sesame seeds.

- Cut each sausage into 12 and put on a lightly greased baking sheet (you'll probably need two sheets, or cook in two batches). Bake for 10-15 minutes until crisp and golden brown. Transfer to a cooling rack. Serve hot or cold.

Carrot
Hotdogs

Carrot Hotdogs

Serves 6 | Prep time 10 minutes | Cook time 20 minutes

Ingredients

6 medium, evenly sized carrots, peeled and trimmed

250ml vegetable stock

2 cloves garlic, peeled and finely chopped

50ml apple cider vinegar

2 tablespoons soya sauce

2 teaspoons maple syrup

1 teaspoon liquid smoke

3 teaspoons smoked paprika

1 teaspoon black pepper

1 tablespoon olive oil

2 medium onions, peeled and finely sliced

6 hotdog rolls

American or mild English mustard

Tomato sauce

Method

• In a large heavy-based saucepan, mix together the vegetable stock, garlic, vinegar, soya sauce, liquid smoke, paprika and the black pepper. Add the carrots.

• Gently bring the carrots to the boil, cover, then reduce the heat to low. Let the carrots cook very slowly for about 30 minutes. The stock should be at a bare simmer, otherwise the carrots will overcook. Turn off the heat and allow the carrots to cool in the stock.

Hotdogs remind me of when the fair used to come to town, the ride operators shouting, organ music, people screaming, candyfloss and the heady smell of frying onions. These are definitely the healthier option but taste easily as good, if not better.

- Heat half the oil in a frying pan. When hot, add the onions and cook, allowing them to brown slightly. Remove from the pan and set aside.

- Heat the rest of the oil in the pan over medium to high heat and add the carrots. Cook for about 5 minutes, turning regularly, until browning slightly all the way around.

- Cut the hotdog buns three-quarters of the way through from top to bottom. Place a carrot in each. Quickly return the onions to the pan to reheat.

- Top the carrots with fried onions and criss-cross with a squeeze of mustard and tomato sauce.

Sunny Dogs

Sunny Dogs

Makes 6 | Prep time 20 minutes | Cook time 25 minutes

Ingredients

For the sweet corn relish

2 cobs of sweet corn

1 medium onion, peeled and finely diced

½ red pepper, finely diced

½ red chilli, finely chopped

25g golden caster sugar

75ml white wine vinegar

1 teaspoon ready made English mustard

Pinch salt

For the dogs

1 tablespoon rapeseed oil

150g chickpeas, soaked overnight with ½ teaspoon bicarbonate of soda, or 1 x 400g tin chickpeas, drained

1 medium onion, chopped

2-3 cloves garlic, peeled and roughly chopped

1 teaspoon cumin

Bunch parsley, roughly chopped

1 bunch coriander, roughly chopped

1 teaspoon tahini

¼ teaspoon chilli powder

2 tablespoons gram flour (basan)

Sea salt and black pepper

6 teaspoons sesame seeds

6 hotdog rolls

Mixed salad leaves

Method

To make the relish

- Cut the corn from the cobs and combine with all the other relish ingredients in a medium-sized saucepan and simmer gently, stirring occasionally, for 15-20 minutes, until tender. Pour into a pretty dish to serve.

For the dogs

- Put the chickpeas, onion, garlic, parsley, coriander, tahini and chilli powder in a food processor and pulse until well combined. Mix in the flour and season.

- Divide the mixture into 6 and with wet hands roll each piece in a teaspoonful of seeds to make a tube shape.

- Heat the oil in a large frying pan over medium to high heat.

- Fry the dogs, turning gently and carefully, until browned all round – about 10 minutes. Put the dogs in the hot dog rolls with the mixed salad leaves, top with relish and serve.

I love this combination, the relish works so well with the dogs. It's sure to be a winner.

Sweet Snacks

Honeycomb Popcorn

Honeycomb Popcorn

Serves 4 | Prep time 15 minutes | Cook time 20 minutes

Ingredients

75g golden caster sugar

2 tablespoons golden syrup

1 teaspoon bicarbonate of soda

½ tablespoon rapeseed oil

150g popping corn

Sea salt

This is such fun to make and eat, and the contrast in textures and sweet and salty flavours add to the fun!

Method

- To make the honeycomb, oil a large baking tray and set aside.

- Over very gentle heat, melt the sugar and syrup for about 20 minutes, stirring occasionally, until the sugar has completely dissolved.

- Turn the heat up to medium, watch carefully, but do not stir or move the pan – the mixture will turn a rich golden colour. Turn off the heat and immediately add the bicarbonate of soda, whisk just to combine and quickly pour into the centre of the oiled baking tray. Don't spread it out or move the pan – just leave to completely cool (about 30 minutes).

- Whilst the honeycomb is cooling, heat the oil in a large saucepan, tip in the popping corn and cover. After about 1 minute the corn will start popping – shake the pan occasionally. When the popping stops, take off the lid and sprinkle with a little salt.

- Break the honeycomb into shards and serve in cones with the popcorn for the perfect snack whilst watching a film!

Coconut and Peanut Butter Cookies

Coconut and Peanut Butter Cookies

Makes 20 | Prep time 30 minutes | Cook time 15 minutes

Ingredients

1 tablespoon ground flax seeds

3 tablespoons water

200g self-raising flour

½ teaspoon bicarbonate of soda

½ teaspoon fine sea salt

75g non-dairy butter

125g soft brown sugar

125g crunchy peanut butter

25g desiccated coconut

1 teaspoon vanilla extract

For decoration

Peanut halves

Desiccated coconut

Method

• Mix the flaxseed with the water and set aside to thicken for a few minutes. In a large mixing bowl, sift together the flour and bicarbonate of soda and mix in the salt. In another mixing bowl, cream together the butter, sugar and peanut butter. Stir in the desiccated coconut, vanilla extract and the flaxseed mixture until well combined.

• Add the dry mixture and bring everything together to make a dough.

• Allow to rest in the fridge for about 20 minutes.

• Preheat the oven to 180°C.

• Break the dough into walnut-sized pieces, roll each piece into a ball, flatten into a circle, use a fork to crisscross a pattern on the top.

- Top half the cookies with desiccated coconut and the other half with peanut halves. Press gently into the cookies.

- Transfer the cookies to a couple of baking sheets – don't overcrowd, as they spread during cooking.

- Bake for 12-14 minutes. Remove to a cooling rack to cool.

If they don't all get gobbled up straight away, they keep well in an airtight container.

Chocolate and Pecan Fudge

Makes 20 | Prep time 5 minutes | Cook time 10 minutes
Cooling 4 hours

Ingredients

75ml plant-based milk (e.g. soya, almond, etc.)

50g icing sugar

75ml coconut milk (from the top of a can of full-fat coconut milk)

35g non-dairy butter

500g dark chocolate, broken into small pieces

50g pecans, chopped

20 pecan halves

Method

- Grease and line a 20 x 20cm baking tin.

- In a medium-sized saucepan, mix the plant based milk with the icing sugar until smooth. Add all the other ingredients apart from the pecan halves.

- Stir over gentle heat until everything has melted and combined, about 10 minutes. Pour into the prepared baking tin. Top with the pecan halves evenly spaced and refrigerate for 4 hours.

- Cut into squares. They will keep in an airtight container in the fridge for 2-3 weeks.

Well, if you're looking for the perfect end to your meal, this is it!

Maple Joys

Makes 24 | Prep time 10 minutes | Cook time 10 minutes

Ingredients

100g non-dairy butter

50g soft brown sugar

1 tablespoon maple syrup

200g cornflakes

Method

- Preheat the oven to 160°C.

- Line 2 fairy cake trays with paper cases.

- In a medium-sized saucepan over medium heat, melt the butter, sugar and maple syrup.

- When fully melted, pour over the cornflakes in a large mixing bowl. Stir to combine all the ingredients well.

- Spoon the mixture into the paper cases and bake in the oven for about 10 minutes.

- Allow to cool in the tins before removing.

Cornflake or rice crispy cakes are often the first thing children can make on their own. They are served at seemingly every child's birthday party and are universally loved. Joyous simplicity.

Doughnut Peach Burgers

Doughnut Peach Burgers

Makes 8 | Prep time 15 minutes | Cook time 40 minutes

Ingredients

8 doughnut peaches

250g self-raising flour

350g soft brown sugar

½ teaspoon baking powder

1 teaspoon salt

65g cocoa powder

100ml orange juice

150ml water

250ml vegetable oil

1 teaspoon vanilla essence

Method

• Preheat the oven to 200°C.

• In a large mixing bowl, combine the flour, sugar, baking powder, salt and cocoa powder.

• Stir in the orange juice, water, oil and vanilla essence until all well combined.

• Pour the mixture into a baking tin, approximately 23 x 33cm, and bake in the oven for about 30 minutes. Leave to cool in the tin.

• Cut the peaches in half horizontally and carefully remove the stone, which should slip out quite easily.

• Using a cookie cutter the same size as the peaches (about 8cm), cut the brownies into 8 discs. Remove carefully from the tin, using a fish slice to help, place each brownie disc on top of the peach halves and top with the other half to make a burger.

It is a bit whacky, but I guarantee these will be a hit with children of all sizes! It's fun food! I think food should be fun, taken seriously enough to be delicious, but not so seriously that you suck the fun out of preparing and eating it. Make these and smile!

Minty Lime Bars

Minty Lime Bars

Makes 8 | Prep time 45 minutes | Cook time 20 minutes

Ingredients

150g ginger nut biscuits

75g non-dairy butter, melted

125g cashew nuts, soaked in boiling water for 1 hour

125g coconut milk (the hard part at the top of the tin)

2 tablespoons cornflour

2 tablespoons maple syrup

2 tablespoons icing sugar

2 limes, juice and zest

1 teaspoon peppermint essence

1 teaspoon green food colouring (optional)

Suggestions for decorating

Mint chocolates

Melted dark chocolate

Mint leaves

Green icing

These are so easy to make, and decorating can be as simple or as state of the art as you want.

Method

- Preheat the oven to 170°C.

- Whizz the ginger nut biscuits in a food processor and then add the melted butter. Press into a 20 x 20cm baking tray and set aside in the fridge.

- Put the drained cashew nuts, coconut milk, cornflour, maple syrup, icing sugar, lime juice, peppermint and colouring into a food processor and blitz until really smooth.

- Pour into the base and bake in the oven for about 15-20 minutes, until just set.

- Allow to cool, refrigerate for a couple of hours, then cut into bars. Drizzle with melted chocolate and decorate as desired.

Skittle Brittle

Serves 6 | Prep time 10 minutes | Cook time 20 minutes

Ingredients

100g dairy- free butter

125g golden caster sugar

2 teaspoons vanilla extract

½ teaspoon salt

250g plain flour

75g pecans, chopped

100g Skittles

Method

- Preheat the oven to 160°C.

- In a medium-sized saucepan, gently melt the butter and sugar over low to medium heat. Beat well with a wooden spoon, then add in the vanilla extract, salt, flour and nuts. Press the dough into a baking sheet in a very thin layer. Top with the skittles and gently press them in.

- Bake in the oven for 20-25 minutes.

- Allow to cool completely, then remove from the tin and break into pieces and serve as biscuits with a milkshake, or as a colourful crunchy topping to ice cream.

- They keep well in an airtight container.

Welsh Cakes

Makes 16 | Prep time 20 minutes | Cook time 30 minutes

Ingredients

450g plain flour

2 teaspoons baking powder

225g dairy-free butter

175g golden caster sugar

1 teaspoon ground mixed spice

Pinch salt

175g currants

150ml soya milk (approximately)

Method

- Rub together the flour, baking powder, butter, caster sugar, mixed spice and salt until you have a fine breadcrumb texture.

- Stir in the currants and most of the milk and draw the mixture together with your hand to make a soft dough, adding a little more of the milk if the dough seems dry.

- Tip the dough out onto a lightly floured surface, roll out to a thickness of about 2cm and cut into rounds with a fluted cutter.

- Heat a non-stick frying pan over medium heat (without oil) and fry the Welsh cakes for 3-4 minutes on each side until golden brown and cooked through. Cool on a wire rack.

- Sprinkle with icing or caster sugar if you like, and serve with a nice cup of tea.

I think every child growing up in Wales has at some point either made or eaten Welsh cakes. A national treasure for very good reason!

Oktober Muffins

Oktober Muffins

Makes 12 | Prep time 20 minutes | Cook time 25 minutes

Ingredients

For the muffins

2 medium carrots (approx 250g), grated

1 cooking apple (approx 150g), peeled, cored and grated

150g sultanas

50g mixed nuts, chopped

225g plain flour

150g dark brown soft sugar

1 tablespoon maple syrup

1 teaspoon mixed spice

2 teaspoons baking powder

2 teaspoons egg replacer (I use Orgran No Egg)

For the topping

200g non-dairy cream cheese

200g non-dairy butter

250g icing sugar, sifted

Method

- Preheat the oven to 200°C.

- Line a muffin tin with 12 paper cases.

- In a large mixing bowl, mix together the carrots, apple, sultanas, three-quarters of the nuts, flour, sugar, maple syrup, mixed spice, baking powder and the egg replacer mixed to the pack instructions. Mix well and spoon into the muffin cases.

I spent some time working on a farm in Vermont many years ago, where they still harvested maple syrup using draft horses and gathered all their own produce from the garden, and these muffins remind me so much of a New England autumn.

- Bake in the oven for about 20 minutes until golden and springy to the touch. Take out of the tin and place on a cooling rack.

- In the meantime, combine the cream cheese, butter and icing sugar to make the icing. When the muffins are cold, either pipe or simply spread on the icing and sprinkle with the remaining chopped nuts.

Chocolate Blueberry Bombs

Makes 12 | Prep time 20 minutes | Cook time 25 minutes

Ingredients

200g dark chocolate

50g pecans, chopped

250g blueberries

This is a sure winner for children's lunch boxes, or for after-dinner treats.

Method

• Melt the chocolate in a bowl over a saucepan of simmering water on the stove.

• Gently fold in the blueberries and most of the chopped pecans, reserving some to sprinkle on the top.

• Put a sheet of baking parchment or greaseproof paper on a large plate or baking sheet and spoon on several mounds of the mixture (about 12), or alternatively into petit four cases.

• Top with the reserved pecans. Refrigerate for about 4 hours before serving.

Most dark chocolate is dairy-free, but check the ingredients list.

With blueberries being a superfood with so many health benefits, protein in the nuts and the feel-good factor of chocolate, these little bombs deliver on every level. They are the bomb!

Mains

Babs 'n' Tots

Babs 'n' Tots

Serves 4 | Prep time 1 hour | Cook time 45 minutes

Ingredients

For the babs

1 tablespoon rapeseed oil

400g sweet potato, peeled and cut into chunks

350g carrots, peeled and cut into chunks

2 green peppers, cut into chunks

2 medium onions, peeled and cut into chunks

2 large vine-ripened tomatoes, cut into 6 wedges each

For the marinade

3 tablespoons Hoisin sauce

1 tablespoon tomato sauce

1 tablespoon marmalade

1 tablespoon toasted sesame seeds

2 teaspoons ready-made English mustard.

For the tots

1kg potatoes, peeled and cut into chunks

1 medium onion, peeled and very finely diced

Small bunch of parsley, chopped

½ teaspoon paprika

1 tablespoon plain flour

Sea salt and black pepper

Sunflower oil for deep frying

For the dip

4 tablespoons vegan mayonnaise

Method

No cutlery required, great party finger food.

- Parboil the potatoes for about 10 minutes, until just starting to soften. Drain and set aside until cool enough to handle, then grate (using a box grater, not by machine, as they'll become very sticky).

- Gently fry off the onions until soft but not browned and stir in the parsley and papika. Mix into the grated potatoes with the flour and season well.

- On a floured board, roll the potato mixture into a long sausage and cut into 1.5cm pieces. Set aside on a plate in the fridge until ready to cook.

- Preheat the oven to 200°C.

To make the babs
- String all the vegetables onto skewers, alternating them as you go so that each skewer has an equal amount. Drizzle with oil and bake in the oven for about 20 minutes.

Babs 'n' Tots

In the meantime make the marinade

- Whisk all the ingredients together in a small mixing bowl. (Reserve about 2-3 teaspoonful to add to the mayonnaise for the dip.)

- Baste the kebabs with the marinade and cook for a further 10-20 minutes, basting from time to time until the vegetables are soft.

- Heat the oil for deep frying and fry the tots in a few batches for about 5 minutes until golden and crispy. Drain on kitchen roll, sprinkle with sea salt and serve with the babs and dip.

- If the carrots and sweet potato are difficult to thread onto the skewers, make a hole in them first using the point of a small knife.

Chinese Takeaway Curry with Noodles

Serves 4 | Prep time 20 minutes | Cook time 20 minutes

Ingredients

1 tablespoon rapeseed oil

2 medium onions, finely sliced

250g carrots, peeled and cut into rings

400g potatoes, peeled and cut into 2cm dice

3 cloves garlic, finely diced

2 dessert apples, peeled and grated

50g golden sultanas

200g Chinese curry sauce concentrate (e.g. Goldfish brand), dissolved in 600ml boiling water

100g frozen edamame beans

4 spring onions, sliced on the diagonal

To serve

Soy sauce

Chilli flakes

Toasted sesame seeds

400g Chinese flat noodles

Chinese Takeaway Curry with Noodles

Method

- In a large heavy-based saucepan, heat the oil over medium heat, add the onions, carrots, potatoes and garlic, cover and cook gently, stirring from time to time, for about 10 minutes.

- When the vegetables are cooked but still firm, add the apple, raisins and curry sauce. Simmer for about 5 minutes, add the edamame beans and spring onions, cover and simmer for a further 5 minutes.

- Bring a large saucepan of water to the boil and cook the noodles according to the packet instructions.

- When the noodles are cooked, drain and divide between four bowls, spoon over the curry and serve with soy sauce, chilli flakes and toasted sesame seeds.

Living where I do, eight miles from the nearest town, we very rarely have takeaways, as it is usually cold by the time we get it home, but who doesn't love a Chinese takeaway?
I know it defeats the object of a takeaway by making it at home, but if, like me, you live a bit off the beaten track and your nearest Chinese is not that accessible, this is just the job for a cold, windy and rainy night watching a film curled up on the settee!
Serve in takeaway cartons and eat with chopsticks for the real deal!

Spaghetti Caulinese

Spaghetti Caulinese

Serves 4 | Prep time 20 minutes | Cook time 40 minutes

Ingredients

1 medium cauliflower, leaves removed

4-5 sprigs fresh oregano, stalks removed

2 bay leaves

4 cloves

2 teaspoons mixed herbs

1 tablespoon rapeseed oil

Sea salt and black pepper

2 medium onions, peeled and diced

4 cloves garlic, peeled and finely chopped

1 red pepper, sliced

2 medium carrots, grated

½ teaspoon chilli powder

2 tins chopped tomatoes

1 vegetable stock cube

100g tomato purée

500g dried spaghetti

To make a pretend Parmesan-like topping

In a blender, whiz together:

75g cashew nuts

2 tablespoons nutritional yeast and

Pinch garlic granules

Roasting the cauliflower first brings out a delicious depth of flavour.

Method

- Preheat the oven to 220°C.

- Firstly, chop the cauliflower into small pieces (use the stalk too) and put in a large roasting tin with the oregano, bay leaves, cloves, mixed herbs, rapeseed oil and seasoning. Mix to coat everything in the oil and bake for about 20 minutes until the cauliflower is just starting to brown and has softened.

- In the meantime, in a large heavy-based saucepan, heat the oil over a medium to high heat and add the onions, garlic, red pepper, carrots and chilli powder. Fry, stirring from time to time, for 10-15 minutes until everything is soft.

- Add the tomatoes, tomato purée and crumble in the stock cube. Bring to the boil, then reduce to a simmer for about 20 minutes.

- Stir in the cauliflower (reserving 2 tablespoons for garnish). Season well. Cook the spaghetti according to the packet instructions, drain and pile into warm bowls and then ladle on the caulinese sauce and top with the remaining roasted cauliflower.

Peter Rabbit's
Forage Bowl

Peter Rabbit's Forage Bowl

Serves 2-4 | Prep time 20 minutes | Cook time 0 minutes

Ingredients

For the salad

20 very young, fresh dandelion leaves

2 little gem lettuce, shredded

1 medium red apple, unpeeled and sliced

1 medium carrot, cut into ribbons with a peeler

Handful fenugreek sprouts/alfalfa or beansprouts

75g red cabbage, shredded

25g mixed seeds (e.g. pumpkin, sunflower, linseed etc.)

25g hazelnuts, roughly chopped

For the dressing

50g raspberries

2 tablespoons extra virgin olive oil

2-3 teaspoons elderberry or red wine vinegar

1 teaspoon golden caster sugar

Sea salt and freshly ground black pepper

To garnish

10-12 red clover flowers

I love foraging for food. Fresh and free, what could be better. Make sure the dandelion leaves are young and tender, as they do become bitter with age.

Method

- The fenugreek sprouts require a little bit of forethought! Put about 25g of fenugreek seeds in a large jar or mixing bowl. No fancy equipment is required at all.

- Cover the seeds with cold water and leave on a windowsill for about 12 hours. Using a sieve, drain the seeds, rinse in cold water, strain and return to the jar or bowl. Cover loosely with a tea towel or dish cloth.

- Repeat the rinsing and straining process twice a day for about five days, or until your sprouts have grown well and are starting to turn green on the ends. Once sprouted, the sprouts will stay fresh in the fridge for several days.

- Toast the hazelnuts in a small, dry frying pan over medium to high heat for a few minutes. Set aside to cool.

- Mix all the salad ingredients in a large pretty serving dish and scatter the hazelnuts on top. Mix all the dressing ingredients, season and sieve to remove the raspberry seeds. Pour the dressing over the salad, toss lightly and garnish with Peter's favourite, the red clover flowers!

Little Lentil Noodle Nest

Little Lentil Noodle Nest

Serves 4 | Prep time 20 minutes | Cook time 25 minutes

Ingredients

150g green lentils

1l water

1 vegetable stock cube

4 medium tomatoes, blanched, peeled and pips removed

2 carrots, peeled and sliced

1 stick celery, finely sliced

1 apple, peeled, cored and grated

100g frozen peas

2 large cloves garlic, peeled and finely chopped

1 tablespoon olive oil

1 tablespoon barbecue sauce

1 teaspoon smoked paprika

1 tablespoon tomato purée

Black pepper, sea salt

500g pack tagliatelle

When my children were young, I often used to make something very similar to this which eventually became known simply as 'nest', it was a family favourite over the years, and still is!

Method

- Put the lentils, water and stock cube in a large heavy-based saucepan, cover and bring to a rapid boil. Reduce the heat to a simmer and cook for 20 minutes.

- Stir in the other ingredients, increasing the heat a little until boiling, then reduce again to a simmer for 20 minutes.

- Check the seasoning.

- In the meantime, cook the tagliatelle according to the packet instructions, drain, divide into four warmed pasta dishes and ladle the lentils into the middle to make 'nests'. Serve immediately.

Winner Dinner Stinger Slices

Winner Dinner Stinger Slices

Makes 8 | Prep time 20 minutes | Cook time 30 minutes

Ingredients

1 tablespoon rapeseed oil

1 medium onion, peeled and diced

2 medium potatoes, peeled and cut into small dice

200g swede, peeled and cut into small dice

100g young nettle tops, washed and roughly chopped

1 teaspoon mixed herbs

Sea salt and white pepper

2 packs ready rolled puff pastry.

Splash soya milk

Method

• In a medium-sized saucepan, heat the oil, add the onion, potatoes, swede and mixed herbs, reduce the heat to medium, cover and sweat off for 10-15 minutes, stirring occasionally, until the vegetables are soft, but still retain a bit of bite.

• Stir in the nettles and season well. Cover and cook for a further 5 minutes or so, until the nettles have wilted.

• Remove from the heat and allow to cool.

• Preheat the oven to 220°C.

Obviously, take care when picking the nettles, but cooking completely disarms them. I have plenty of nettles in my garden; they are not just wonderful to eat, but attract an array of wildlife. There is something mysteriously magical about them.

- Cut each sheet of pastry into four rectangles. Fill each rectangle with about a tablespoon of the mixture, brush the edges with a little soya milk, fold in half and press the edges down with a fork to seal. Brush the tops with a little more soya milk.

- Put on a lightly greased baking tray and bake in the oven for about 15 minutes, or until puffed up and golden brown.

- Eat hot or cold.

Allotment Pie

Serves 6-8 | Prep time 30 minutes | Cook time 1 hour

Ingredients

For the topping

1.5kg potatoes, peeled and roughly chopped

150ml soya milk

100g non-dairy butter

Sea salt, ground white pepper

1 packet plain crisps, crushed

1 tablespoon nutritional yeast

1 teaspoon paprika

For the filling

1 tablespoon rapeseed oil

2 medium onions, peeled and diced

3 cloves garlic, peeled and finely chopped

2 medium carrots, peeled and diced

½ small swede, peeled and diced

1 stick celery, diced

2 teaspoons dried mixed herbs

½ teaspoon chilli flakes

2 tablespoons plain flour

200g frozen peas

1 x 565g tin jackfruit (in brine), roughly chopped

1 vegetable stock cube

1-2 teaspoons gravy browning

Method

- Put the potatoes in a large heavy-based saucepan, cover with salted water and bring to the boil over high heat. Reduce the heat to a simmer and cook for about 10-15 minutes until soft. Strain and reserve the cooking water in a jug.

Allotment Pie

- Mash the potatoes with the milk and half the butter and season with plenty of white pepper and more salt if it's needed. Set aside.

- Preheat the oven to 200°C.

- In a large heavy-based frying pan, heat the oil, add the onions, garlic, carrots, swede, celery, mixed herbs and chilli flakes and cook over medium heat for about 10 minutes, stirring from time to time.

- Stir in the flour and continue cooking, stirring often, for a further 2-3 minutes. Slowly add about 1 litre of the reserved potato water and keep stirring so that no lumps form. Add the stock cube.

- Stir in the peas and jackfruit and add a small amount of gravy browning, adding a little more as you go until you have a nice dark golden gravy colour. Simmer gently for 5 minutes.

- Put the mixture into a deep ovenproof pie dish, spoon on the mashed potato and use a fork to spread it over the filling so that it is completely covered. Make a pattern on the top with the fork, dot with the remaining butter and sprinkle on the nutritional yeast, the crushed crisps and paprika.

- Bake in the oven for about 30-40 minutes until bubbling and golden brown.

A wonderful winter warmer, a meal in itself, but an accompaniment of some simply steamed greens, such as cabbage, broccoli or leeks, would gild the lily!

Farl and
Jerky Beans

Farl and Jerky Beans

Serves 2 | Prep time 20 minutes | Cook time 30 minutes

Ingredients

For the farl

4 medium potatoes (about 600g), peeled and chopped

1 teaspoon salt

1 tablespoon olive oil

300g plain flour

1 tablespoon fresh chives, snipped

Ground white pepper and sea salt

For the beans

250g green beans, topped and tailed

½ tablespoon rapeseed oil

1 medium onion, peeled and finely sliced

2 cloves garlic, peeled and finely chopped

1 tin chopped tomatoes

2 teaspoons allspice

½ teaspoon cinnamon

½ teaspoon freshly

Grated nutmeg

2 teaspoons soft brown sugar

4-5 sprigs thyme, stalks removed, chopped

Pinch chilli powder

Sea salt and black pepper

The word 'farl' derives from an old Scottish word meaning a quarter. These potato farls are also great as part of a breakfast, or topped with baked beans.

Method

- Boil the potatoes in salted water for about 15 minutes until soft. Drain well and mash with the olive oil and plenty of ground white pepper.

- Stir in the flour and chives and form into a ball. Turn out onto a floured surface and with your hands shape the mixture into a flat 9-inch circle. Cut the circle into quarters. In a large heavy-based frying pan, fry the farls (no oil needed) over medium heat for about 10 minutes on each side until golden brown.

- In the meantime, cook the beans in boiling water for about 3-4 minutes, until cooked but still retaining some bite. Drain and plunge into cold water. Set aside.

- In a frying pan, heat the oil and fry the onions and garlic over medium to high heat for about 5 minutes until soft, stirring occasionally.

- Add the tomatoes, spices, thyme and sugar. Simmer for about 10 minutes, mix in the beans to heat though and serve with the farls.

Black Eye Bean Sloppy Joes

Black Eye Bean Sloppy Joes

Serves 6 | Prep time 20 minutes | Cook time 25 minutes

Ingredients

1 tablespoon olive oil

2 medium onions, peeled and finely diced

2 medium carrots, peeled and finely diced

1 red pepper, finely diced

1 red chilli, finely diced

3 cloves garlic, peeled and finely chopped

1 teaspoon fresh thyme, chopped

2 x 400g tins black-eyed beans, or 400g dried beans soaked overnight, rinsed and boiled for 40 minutes until soft

1 tablespoon black treacle

2 tablespoons tomato purée

2 tablespoons white wine vinegar

1 tablespoon soya sauce

1 teaspoon liquid smoke

Sea salt, black pepper

To serve

6 burger buns, toasted

Shredded lettuce

Gherkins, sliced

Red onion, finely sliced into rings

Sloppy Joes originated in Sioux City, Iowa in the 1930s. They were the brainchild of a chef by the name of, yes, you guessed it, Joe!

Method

- Heat the olive oil in a large heavy based frying pan over medium to high heat, add the onions, carrots, pepper, chilli, garlic and thyme, reduce the heat and cook gently for about 15 minutes, stirring occasionally, until everything is soft.

- In a medium-sized mixing bowl, combine the treacle, tomato purée, vinegar, soya sauce and liquid smoke.

- When all the vegetables are cooked and soft, add the black eyed beans and the treacle mixture. Cook over low to medium heat for 5-10 minutes until everything is piping hot. Season with salt and pepper.

- Put some shredded lettuce on each toasted burger bun bottom, top with the sloppy joe, sliced onions and gherkins, top with the toasted bun top and serve immediately.

Hugely popular in the States, this is my version that I'm pretty pleased with.

The Big Red
with Dumplets

The Big Red with Dumplets

Serves 6 | Prep time 45 mins | Cook time 1 hour 30 mins

Ingredients

For roasting

2 tablespoons rapeseed oil

2 medium red onions, peeled and cut into quarters

6 cloves garlic, peeled and finely chopped

1 celery stalk, chopped

3 medium carrots, unpeeled, cut into chunks

4 medium beetroot, unpeeled, cut into chunks

2 medium sweet potatoes, unpeeled, cut into chunks

2 red peppers, cut into chunks

12 baby potatoes, unpeeled, cut in half

2-3 vine-ripened tomatoes, cut into quarters

1-2 red chillies, sliced

2-3 teaspoons dried mixed herbs

Black pepper and sea salt

For the next stage

½ medium red cabbage, shredded

2 x 400g tins chopped tomatoes

1 x 400g tin red kidney beans

1 tablespoon dark brown sugar

2 tablespoons red wine vinegar

1 teaspoon red chilli powder

1 vegetable stock cube dissolved in 600ml boiling water

100g tomato purée

For the dumplets

150g split red lentils

125g self-raising flour

1 teaspoon cumin

1 teaspoon coriander powder

1 teaspoon turmeric

Sea salt

Method

- Preheat the oven to 220°C.

- Put the oil and all the roasting vegetables in a large roasting tray and roast for about 45 minutes until everything is soft and cooked.

- Stir in the second list of ingredients and return to the oven for 20-25 minutes, stirring occasionally.

- In the meantime, boil the lentils in salted water for about 15 minutes or until just soft, drain and cool under cold running water.

- In a mixing bowl, combine the lentils, flour and spices to make a dough.

- Take the vegetables out of the oven, check the seasoning and add a little more water if needed.

- Divide the dumplets into 20 and dot them over the vegetables. Cover with foil and return to the oven for a further 15 minutes until the dumplets are soft and swollen.

- Serve hot. It's a meal in itself, but some tenderstem broccoli would be a colourful accompaniment.

Filling, wholesome and fun. The colours are incredible. There are lots of ingredients in this recipe, but it is absolutely worth the effort. One of my favourites.

Pizza

Serves 6 | Prep time 30 minutes | Cook time 10-30 minutes

Ingredients

For the dough

300g strong white bread flour

7g dried active yeast

7g salt

1 tablespoon olive oil

200ml lukewarm water

For the tomato topping

1 tablespoon olive oil

1 medium onion, peeled and finely diced

2 cloves garlic, peeled and finely chopped

1 red pepper, finely diced

1 red chilli, finely diced

1 tablespoon fresh herbs, chopped (e.g. oregano, parsley, thyme, marjoram, basil etc)

1 x 400g tin chopped tomatoes

1 tablespoon tomato purée

Sea salt, black pepper

For the vegetable toppings

Choose from: artichoke hearts, sweetcorn, sliced mushrooms, red onion, olives, tender stem broccoli, asparagus, pineapple, sliced chillies, mange tout, spinach etc.

150g grated Violife cheddar (or other plant-based cheddar), grated

A sprinkling semolina

Pizza

Method

- To make the dough, mix the flour, yeast and salt together in a large mixing bowl, add the olive oil and water and bring together with your hand to form a dough. Turn out onto a lightly floured surface and knead for about 5 minutes. Return to the bowl and set aside whilst you prepare the sauce.

- Preheat the oven to 240°C.

- Heat the oil in a large heavy-based frying pan over medium to high heat, add the onions, garlic, pepper and chilli, reduce the heat to medium and cook gently, stirring frequently, for about 15 minutes until everything is very soft but not coloured.

- Add the herbs, tomatoes and tomato purée, simmer for 5-10 minutes until the sauce has reduced and thickened.

Shop-bought pizza pales into insignificance in comparison. If you're looking to make life a bit easier though, use a good quality shop bought pasta sauce instead of making your own.

- Turn the dough out onto a lightly floured surface and divide into two. Roll or stretch each ball into a circle, thinner in the middle and slightly thicker around the outer edges (roughly 30cm across).

- Either using two flat baking sheets or the upturned base of two large roasting trays, sprinkle with semolina and place a pizza base on each.

- Divide the tomato sauce between the two (there may be some left over – don't overload your pizza, as it will become soggy).

- Top with your chosen toppings, then the grated Violife cheddar and cook in the oven for about 10-15 minutes until the crust has risen and browned.

Pepper Pigs and Panzanella

Serves 4 | Prep time 30 minutes | Cook time 15 minutes

Ingredients

For the peppers

4 long, pointy red peppers, cut in half lengthways

1 tablespoon rapeseed oil

240g basmati and wild rice

500ml water

50g pine nuts, toasted

200g baby spinach leaves

75g non-dairy butter

75g plain flour

400ml unsweetened soya milk

2 teaspoons English mustard

1-2 teaspoons paprika

Sea salt and ground white pepper

For the Panzanella

3 tablespoons extra virgin olive oil

200g stale ciabatta, torn into chunks

500g mixed tomatoes, cut into chunks

Handful baby spinach leaves

Large handful fresh basil leaves, torn

1 tablespoon red wine vinegar

1 teaspoon Dijon mustard

Sea salt and black pepper

Pepper Pigs and Panzanella

Method

- Preheat the oven to 220°C.

- In a mixing bowl, coat the ciabatta with the olive oil (retaining the excess oil in the bowl). Spread on a baking sheet and bake in the oven for about 10 minutes until crispy and brown. Set aside. Put the tomatoes in a colander over the bowl with the excess oil, sprinkle with sea salt and set aside.

- Put the peppers on a baking sheet, drizzle with the oil and a little seasoning and cook in the oven for about 10 minutes. Take out and set aside, ready to be filled.

- Put the rice and water in a medium-sized saucepan, salt, cover and bring to the boil. Reduce the heat to a bare simmer for about 15-20 minutes, when nearly all the water has been absorbed and the rice is cooked. Turn the heat off and stir in the spinach until it has wilted,

Summer on a plate! Al fresco in a sunny garden overlooking the sea – perfection!

add the pine nuts and season. Spoon the mixture into the peppers.

- Melt the butter in a medium saucepan over medium heat, stir in the flour. Gradually add the milk, whisking regularly so that no lumps form. Add the mustard, white pepper and salt. Cook gently for about 10 minutes.

- Spoon the sauce over the peppers, sprinkle with paprika and return to the oven for about 10 minutes until bubbling and browned.

- Whilst the peppers are cooking, put the tomatoes, basil and spinach in a pretty serving dish. Whisk the vinegar, Dijon mustard, salt and pepper into the oil and juice that has come from the tomatoes. Toss the ciabatta, salad and dressing together and serve alongside the peppers.

Wild West Hodge Podge and Soda Bread

Wild West Hodge Podge and Soda Bread

Serves 4 | Prep time 20 minutes | Cook time 1 hour

Ingredients

For the bread

350g plain flour

1 teaspoon salt

1 teaspoon bicarbonate of soda

275ml unsweetened soya milk

1 tablespoon apple cider vinegar

For the soup

1 tablespoon rapeseed oil

3 medium red onions, finely diced

2 cloves garlic, peeled and finely diced

2 medium potatoes, peeled and cut into small dice

2 medium sweet potatoes, peeled and cut into small dice

½ tablespoon dark brown soft sugar

1 tablespoon tomato ketchup

1 tablespoon red wine vinegar

1 teaspoon smoked paprika

1 x 400g tin chopped tomatoes

2 x 400g tins baked beans

Sea salt and ground white pepper

Campfire nosh. Perfect for cowboys and Indians of all ages!

Method

- To make the bread, preheat the oven to 200˚C.

- Mix the soya milk and apple cider vinegar in a bowl and allow a couple of minutes to curdle. In the meantime, combine the flour, salt and bicarbonate of soda. Stir in the curdled milk and combine to make a dough.

- Tip out onto a lightly floured surface and shape into a round. Place on a lightly greased baking tray and cut a deep cross in the top. This will help it to cook evenly.

- Bake for about 30 minutes until golden.

- Place on a rack to cool.

- Whilst the bread is cooking, in a large saucepan, heat the oil, then add the onions, garlic, potatoes and sweet potatoes.

- Reduce the heat to low to medium, cover the pan and cook, stirring occasionally, for about 20 minutes.

- Add all the other soup ingredients, season and simmer for a further 20 minutes until everything is soft and cooked through.

- Serve in bowls with big chunks of the soda bread.

Chimichurri Hasselbacks

Chimichurri Hasselbacks

Serves 2 | Prep time 20 minutes | Cook time 45 minutes

Ingredients

2 medium-sized potatoes, washed but unpeeled

2 medium-sized sweet potatoes, washed but unpeeled

2 dessertspoons dairy-free yoghurt

For the chimichurri

Large bunch of parsley

2 tablespoons red wine vinegar

3 tablespoons olive or rapeseed oil

1 red chilli pepper

2 cloves garlic

½ tablespoons fresh (or 2 teaspoons dried) oregano

Sea salt and black pepper

For the stir fry

1 tablespoon rapeseed oil

2 medium onions, finely sliced

1 bag ready prepared kale (or other leafy greens e.g. spinach, cabbage or chard)

Sea salt and black pepper

This dish has a bit of sophistication about it and looks impressive but is dead simple to make. Perfect teenager supper party fare

Method

- Preheat the oven to 200°C.

- Vertically slice the potatoes and sweet potatoes three-quarters of the way through, being careful not to cut fully. Put in a medium-sized roasting dish. For the sauce – chop the parsley in a food processor and then add all the other ingredients and blitz for about a minute.

- Drizzle a teaspoon or two of the sauce over each potato and put in to roast. Keep basting with a little more of the sauce every 10-15 minutes until about half the sauce is used up.

- After about 1 hour, the potatoes should be tender when poked with a knife. Just before you think the potatoes are done, heat the oil in a large frying pan until hot, toss in the onions and stir fry for 2-3 minutes, add the greens, continue to stir fry until wilted and tender. Season.

- To serve, put one potato and one sweet potato on the plate, top with a little more of the sauce and a dessertspoonful of yoghurt, and some of the stir-fried greens on the side.

Beijing Burger, Asian Slaw and Sunomono

Serves 6 | Prep time 45 minutes | Cook time 15 minutes

Ingredients

For the burgers

1 tbsp rapeseed oil

125g edamame beans, cooked

1 x 400g tin black beans, drained

125g courgette, grated

1 medium carrot, grated

50g panko breadcrumbs

50g blanched peanuts, toasted and roughly chopped

½ medium onion, finely chopped

Small bunch coriander, chopped

75g beansprouts, cut in half

2 replacement eggs (I used Orgran No Egg)

1 teaspoon Chinese 5 spice

Sea salt and black pepper

1 tablespoon plain flour

6 rolls or burger buns

12 little gem leaves

For the Asian slaw

2 tablespoons crunchy peanut butter

400g white cabbage, finely shredded

1 red pepper, finely sliced

4 spring onions, sliced on the diagonal

1 large clove garlic, peeled and finely chopped

1 tablespoon soya sauce

1 tablespoon rice vinegar

1 tablespoon sriracha

1 tablespoon chopped chives

1 tablespoon toasted sesame seeds

Pinch salt

Beijing Burger, Asian Slaw and Sunomono

Ingredients

For the sunomono

1 cucumber, peeled

2 tablespoons rice vinegar

½ tablespoon golden caster sugar

1 teaspoon fresh ginger, very finely chopped or grated

1 tablespoon fresh basil, chopped

1 spring onion, finely sliced

½ teaspoon fine sea salt

Method

• Firstly, make the sunomono: cut the cucumber in half lengthwise and slice as thinly as possible into half moons. Mix together all the other ingredients. Pour the dressing over the cucumber, making sure all the pieces are well coated.

• Cover and refrigerate.

• Next, make the slaw: in a large mixing bowl, combine the peanut butter, garlic, salt, soya sauce, vinegar and sriracha. Mix well, then add the other ingredients and refrigerate until ready to serve.

• Next, make the burgers: Put the black beans in a food processor and chop, then add the edamame beans and pulse a few times until chopped but retaining some texture.

- Squeeze as much juice as possible out of the courgette, then, in a large mixing bowl, combine all the ingredients, except for the flour.

- Lightly flour a board or worktop and firmly shape your mixture into six patties. Put the patties on a plate in the fridge for half an hour or so to firm up.

- In a large heavy-based frying pan, fry the patties in the oil over medium to high heat for 5 minutes or so, then turn and fry for another 5 minutes or until they are golden and crispy. Serve in the buns or rolls on the little gem leaves, the Asian slaw, then the burger topped with the sunomono.

An absolute triumph of a burger!

Cakes and Desserts

Mysteriously disappear without trace!

Bermuda Triangles

Makes 14 | Prep time 15 minutes | Cook time 5 minutes

Ingredients

½ pineapple, skin removed

1 mango, stoned and peeled

1 banana, peeled and mashed

1 knob stem ginger in syrup, finely chopped

50g golden sultanas

¼ teaspoon mixed spice

1 tablespoon dark brown soft sugar

1 pack ready made filo pastry

Oil for deep frying

2 tablespoons maple syrup

1 tablespoon icing sugar

Method

- Whizz the pineapple and mango in a food processor, put in a medium-sized mixing bowl with the banana, ginger, sultanas, mixed spice and sugar and mix well.

- Cut the filo sheets in half lengthways.

- Put a dessertspoonful of the mixture in the corner of the pastry and fold it over approximately three times until you end up with triangle shapes. Moisten the final join with a little brush of water so that they stick together.

- Fry in small batches in the deep fat fryer until brown, turn and repeat on the other side. They will only take about two minutes.

- Drizzle a little maple syrup on a plate, place the Bermuda triangles on top and dust with icing sugar.

American Diner Pancakes

Serves 4 | Prep time 10 minutes | Cook time 15 minutes

Ingredients

240ml soya milk

1 tablespoon apple cider vinegar

125g plain flour, sifted

50g golden caster sugar

½ tablespoon baking powder

Pinch salt

250g mixed fresh fruits (e.g. blueberries, cherries, apricots, peaches, etc.)

A few basil leaves to garnish

Maple syrup to serve

Method

• Mix the milk and apple cider vinegar together in a jug.

• In a medium-sized mixing bowl, combine the flour, sugar, baking powder and salt. Whisk in the milk mixture and allow to rest for 5 minutes.

• Heat a large heavy-based frying pan over medium to high heat, then ladle in the batter, making 3-4 at a time, depending on the size of your pan.

• Cook for about 3 minutes, until the top starts to bubble, then turn the pancakes over to cook for a further 2-3 minutes on the other side. When nicely browned, stack on a plate and keep warm until all the pancakes are cooked.

• Top with the fruit and a basil leaf and drizzle with maple syrup. Serve with non-dairy yoghurt for a delicious American-style breakfast.

If lots of my recipes seem to have an American origin, it's because Americans really do seem to know how to make food fun!

Ginger Jewel Cake

Ginger Jewel Cake

Serves 8 | Prep time 25 minutes | Cook time 50 minutes

Ingredients

225g dairy-free butter

225g soft dark brown sugar

100g black treacle

125g golden syrup

125ml soya milk

1 tablespoon apple cider vinegar

350g plain flour

1 teaspoon baking powder

1 teaspoon bicarbonate of soda

1 teaspoon mixed spice

1 teaspoon ground ginger

1 teaspoon grated fresh ginger

For the icing

100g icing sugar

½ orange, juice and zest

100g pistachio nuts, chopped

½ pomegranate, pith removed

Method

- Line a 24cm springform tin with baking parchment or greaseproof paper.

- Preheat the oven to 180°C.

- In a medium-sized saucepan over medium heat, melt the butter, sugar, treacle and syrup. Set aside to cool.

- In a jug, combine the milk and vinegar then leave for a few minutes to curdle.

This is a moist, gingery, very pretty cake which is hard to believe is plant-based. It is really amazing what can be achieved without the use of dairy products.

- In a large mixing bowl, sift the flour, baking powder and bicarbonate of soda. Add the spices and stir to combine.

- Add the milk, vinegar and the melted butter mixture to the flour, mix well and pour into the cake tin. Bake in the oven for about 50 minutes to 1 hour or until a skewer inserted in the middle of the cake comes out clean. Allow to cool in the tin for about 10 minutes before turning out onto a cooling rack.

- Sift the icing sugar into a small mixing bowl and add the orange juice a drop at a time until you have a consistency like thick cream.

- When the cake has completely cooled, gently spread the icing on top, sprinkle with the orange zest, chopped pistachio nuts and the pomegranate seeds.

Mutti's Tutti Frutti Loaf

Mutti's Tutti Frutti Loaf

Makes 1 loaf | Prep time 2 hours 20 mins | Cook time 25 mins

Ingredients

2 tea bags

450ml boiling water

250g mixed fruit (to include sultanas, raisins, glacé cherries, mixed peel, dates)

50g mixed seeds (to include pumpkin, sunflower, linseed, flax)

50g mixed nuts, chopped (to include walnuts, almonds, hazelnuts)

400g strong white bread flour

12g dried active yeast

5g salt

1 teaspoon ground mixed spice

A knob of non-dairy butter

1 tablespoon demerara sugar

Method

- In a large bowl, pour the boiling water onto the tea bags, add the fruit, seeds and nuts to the bowl and allow to steep until it gets cold. Remove the tea bags.

- Add the flour, yeast, salt and mixed spice to the bowl and bring all the ingredients together to make a dough.

Absolutely packed with goodness, and very little added sugar, this makes a great afternoon tea treat.

- Turn the dough out onto a lightly floured worktop and knead for a few minutes. Return the dough to the bowl, cover and leave to rise for about 2 hours.

- Again on a lightly floured worktop gently knead the dough and make into an oblong shape to fit into a lightly greased loaf tin.

- Smear the butter on the top and sprinkle with the sugar. Cover the loaf with a tea towel and leave to rise again for about 20-30 minutes or until well risen.

- Preheat the oven to 220°C.

- Bake the loaf for about 25 minutes. Turn the loaf out of the tin – when you tap the underside it should have a hollow sound. If not, return to the oven for 5 minutes more. Cool on a cooling rack. Serve plain or buttered.

Chocolate Cherry Party Cake

Chocolate Cherry Party Cake

Serves 8-10 | Prep time 25 minutes | Cook time 25 minutes

Ingredients

300ml soya milk

1 tablespoon apple cider vinegar

150g non-dairy butter

3 tablespoons maple syrup

1 teaspoon instant coffee granules

275g plain flour, sifted

175g light soft brown sugar

35g cocoa powder

1 teaspoon bicarbonate of soda

For the filling and topping

150g non-dairy butter

275g icing sugar

40g cocoa powder

3 tablespoons cherry jam

Punnet fresh cherries, pitted

A few crushed biscuits

Method

- Preheat the oven to 180°C.

- Line two 20cm sponge tins with baking parchment or greaseproof paper.

- In a jug, mix together the milk and vinegar and allow to stand for 10 minutes.

- In a medium-sized saucepan over medium heat, melt the butter, maple syrup and coffee granules.

- In a large mixing bowl, combine the flour, sugar, cocoa powder and bicarbonate of soda.

- Add the melted butter mixture and the milk mixture to the dry ingredients and stir gently until just combined. Divide between the two sponge tins and bake for 20-25 minutes or until a skewer inserted in the middle of the cake comes out clean.

- Turn out on a wire rack to cool.

- To make the butter icing, mix all the ingredients together and beat until it is very smooth and no lumps remain.

- When the cake has completely cooled, fill with half the butter icing and the cherry jam. With a palette knife, smooth the remaining half of the icing on top of the cake.

- Decorate with the crushed biscuits and the fresh cherries and candles to make a beautiful birthday cake.

Straightforward to make, yet this cake looks magnificent and tastes utterly, ridiculously delicious!

Jam Steamed Pudding

Jam Steamed Pudding

Serves 6 | Prep time 15 mins | Cook time 2 hours, 15 mins

Ingredients

2 tablespoons jam (any kind)

100g non-dairy butter

100g golden caster sugar

2 tablespoons maple syrup

3 tablespoons non-dairy yoghurt

1 teaspoon vanilla extract

215g self-raising flour

1 tablespoon cornflour

½ teaspoon bicarbonate of soda

Method

- Liberally grease a 2.1 litre pudding basin and put a small square of greaseproof paper in the bottom, and spoon in the jam.

- Boil a kettle full of water.

- Over low heat in a small saucepan melt the butter, caster sugar and maple syrup. Sift the flour, cornflour and bicarbonate of soda into a mixing bowl.

- Add the melted butter mixture, milk, yoghurt and vanilla extract and whisk gently until no lumps remain.

- Pour into the prepared basin. Cover with a square of greaseproof paper with a pleat in it, followed by a square of foil with a pleat in it to allow for expansion. Tie tightly with string so none of the steam can get into the pudding and make it soggy.

- Put the pudding in a fairly big saucepan on an upturned saucer. Fill the saucepan with boiling water from the kettle to about halfway up the side of the pudding and simmer gently for at least 2 hours, preferably 15 minutes longer. Check the water level halfway through the cooking time and top up if necessary.

- At the end of the cooking time, carefully lift from the saucepan and remove the string and covers. Place a plate over the pudding and invert so the pudding tips out onto the plate. Serve steaming hot with some extra warmed jam and custard or ice-cream.

These old-fashioned puddings definitely stand the test of time. I remember getting off the bus after school, running home down the lane and praying that Granny had made steamed pudding for tea! This one is as delicious as I remember them to be from years ago.

Carnival Cake

Carnival Cake

Serves 8-10 | Prep time 30 minutes | Cook time 35 minutes

Ingredients

400g plain flour

200g golden caster sugar

1½ teaspoons baking powder

300ml soya milk

150ml rapeseed oil

1 teaspoon vanilla essence

200ml aquafaba

½ teaspoon cream of tartar

70g 100s and 1000s

150g non-dairy butter

325g icing sugar

1 teaspoon vanilla essence

½ lemon, juiced

Method

- Preheat the oven to 180°C.

- Line two 20cm sponge tins with baking parchment or greaseproof paper.

- In a large mixing bowl, whisk together the flour, sugar, baking powder, milk, oil and vanilla essence to make a batter.

- In another large mixing bowl, whisk the aquafaba and cream of tartar using an electric whisk to form soft peaks. This will probably take at least 5 minutes.

- Fold the aquafaba meringue into the batter, being careful not to overwork, as the air will be knocked out of the mixture. On the final few folds mix in about half of the 100s and 1000s, and then immediately divide the batter between the two sponge tins. It's important to do this fairly quickly otherwise the colours in the sponge mix will blend and it will not look quite so pretty.

- Bake in the oven for about 35 minutes or until a skewer inserted into the middle of the cake comes out clean.

- Turn the sponges out and cool on a cooling rack.

- Beat the butter, icing sugar and vanilla essence together in a medium-sized mixing bowl until it is light and smooth, then add a little lemon juice until you have the desired consistency and taste.

- When the sponge has completely cooled, fill with the butter icing. There will be enough icing to cover the top and sides as well. Decorate with the remaining 100s and 1000s.

This lovely light cake could be decorated for any occasion or celebration, for example, a birthday or christening.

Mango Mousse and Shortbread

Mango Mousse and Shortbread

Serves 4 | Prep time 15 minutes | Cook time 15 minutes

Ingredients

For the mousse

2 ripe mangoes, roughly chopped

125g cashew nuts, soaked in boiling water for 1 hour

2 tablespoons maple syrup

1 teaspoon almond essence

1 lemon, juice and zest

2 tablespoons coconut milk (from top of the tin)

Pinch salt

4 teaspoons non-dairy yoghurt

75g blueberries

4 mint leaves

For the shortbread

100g non-dairy butter

½ teaspoon almond essence

50g golden caster sugar

150g plain flour

Method

- Put the strained cashew nuts, mangoes, maple syrup, almond essence, lemon juice and zest, coconut cream and salt into a food processor and blitz on full speed for a few minutes, stopping to scrape down the sides so that everything is really smooth.

- Pour the mixture into four cups, jam jars or glasses and put in the fridge.

- To make the shortbread put all the ingredients into a medium mixing bowl and mix all together until a ball is formed. Wrap in cling film and rest in the fridge for about 1 hour.

- Preheat the oven to 170°C.

- Put the dough onto a lightly floured work top and roll out to about 0.75cm thickness. Cut rounds out with a fluted 6cm cutter. Squeeze together any remaining dough and roll out and cut again until all the dough is used up. Makes approximately 20 biscuits.

- Line a baking sheet with baking parchment or greaseproof paper and bake the biscuits, sprinkled with a little extra sugar, for about 15 minutes. They should be a light golden colour. Cool on a cooling rack.

- To decorate the mousse, top each with a teaspoon of yoghurt, sprinkle on the blueberries and finish with a mint leaf. Serve with the shortbread.

These little shortbread biscuits are so versatile and keep for ages in an airtight container. Crushed up, they make a lovely decoration on the cherry chocolate cake, or to add a bit of texture in the doughnut peach burgers. Or simply serve them with a nice cup of tea!

Banana Butterscotch Sundae

Serves 2 | Prep time 15 minutes | Cook time 5 minutes

Ingredients

50g soft dark brown
sugar

50g dairy-free butter

100ml coconut milk

Pinch salt

½ packet Oreo cookies,
broken into pieces

2 bananas, diced

4 scoops any flavour
dairy-free ice-cream

4 tablespoons dairy-free
yoghurt

2 tablespoons any soft
fruit e.g. blueberries,
raspberries,
strawberries

1 tablespoon walnuts,
chopped

To decorate

Mint or basil leaves,
chocolate drops or 100s
and 1000s

Method

- To make the sauce, combine the butter, sugar, coconut milk and pinch of salt in a saucepan and heat gently, stirring occasionally, until everything has melted, about 5 minutes. Leave to cool. Once the sauce is cold, alternate layers of Oreo cookies, bananas, ice-cream, yogurt and soft fruit between two sundae glasses. Top with the sauce, chopped nuts and one of the other decorations.

- Serve straight away.

Sticky Toffee Apple Pudding

Sticky Toffee Apple Pudding

Serves 6 | Prep time 30 minutes | Cook time 30 minutes

Ingredients

For the pudding

200g dates, roughly chopped

275ml soya milk

75ml water

1 teaspoon bicarbonate of soda

125g non-dairy butter

125g soft dark brown sugar

225g self-raising flour

1 teaspoon vanilla extract

1 teaspoon mixed spice

200g walnuts, toasted and chopped (leaving a few whole for garnish)

For the sauce

75g non-dairy butter

4 apples, peeled, cored and sliced

100g dark soft brown sugar

75g golden caster sugar

225ml coconut milk

1 teaspoon vanilla extract

Pinch salt

Method

- Line a 20cm cake tin with greaseproof paper, or baking parchment.

- Preheat the oven to 200°C.

- In a small saucepan, heat the dates, soya milk and water and simmer for about 5 minutes. Remove from the heat and stir in the bicarbonate of soda – it will froth up. Allow to cool a little. In a medium-sized mixing bowl, beat together the butter, sugar and vanilla extract. Mix in the date mixture to make a batter.

- Fold in the flour, mixed spice and the chopped walnuts. Pour into the lined cake tin and bake for about 25-35 minutes until a skewer poked into the middle of the pudding comes out clean. Whilst the pudding is baking, make the sauce.

- In a medium-sized saucepan, melt the butter and add the apples and cook gently over medium heat for about 5 minutes. Add the sugars and increase the heat a little. After about 10 minutes, when the sugars have melted and taken on a rich golden colour, remove from the heat and stir in the vanilla extract, pinch of salt and the coconut milk.

- When the pudding is cooked, remove from the tin, poke several holes in the top and spoon over about half of the sauce so that it soaks in.

- Garnish with the remaining walnuts and serve with the rest of the sauce and a dollop of soya yoghurt or ice cream.

Utterly indulgent, everything a good pudding should be, and ticks all the boxes.

Metric and imperial equivalents

Weights	Solid		Volume	Liquid
15g	½oz		15ml	½ floz
25g	1oz		30ml	1 floz
40g	1½oz		50ml	2 floz
50g	1¾oz		100ml	3½ floz
75g	2¾oz		125ml	4 floz
100g	3½oz		150ml	5 floz (¼ pint)
125g	4½oz		200ml	7 floz
150g	5½oz		250ml	9 floz
175g	6oz		300ml	10 floz (½ pint)
200g	7oz		400ml	14 floz
250g	9oz		450ml	16 floz
300g	10½oz		500ml	18 floz
400g	14oz		600ml	1 pint (20 floz)
500g	1lb 2oz		1 litre	1¾ pints
1kg	2lb 4oz		1.2 litre	2 pints
1.5kg	3lb 5oz		1.5 litre	2¾ pints
2kg	4lb 8oz		2 litres	3½ pints
3kg	6lb 8oz		3 litres	5¼ pints